The NCTE High School Literature Series

■ ■

Volumes in the Series

Alice Walker in the Classroom

■ ■

"Living by the Word"

The NCTE High School Literature Series

Carol Jago

Santa Monica High School

NATIONAL COUNCIL OF TEACHERS OF ENGLISH
1111 W. KENYON ROAD, URBANA, ILLINOIS 61801-1096

Staff Editor: Rita D. Disroe
Interior Design: Jenny Jensen Greenleaf
Cover Design: Jenny Jensen Greenleaf and Tom Jaczak

NCTE Stock Number: 01143-3050
ISSN 1525-5786

Library of Congress Cataloging-in-Publication Data
Jago, Carol, 1951–
    Alice Walker in the classroom: living by the word/ Carol Jago.
        p. cm.—(The NCTE high school literature series, ISSN 1525-5786)
    Includes bibliographical references (p.).
    ISBN 0-8141-0114-3
    1. Walker, Alice, 1944—Study and teaching. 2. Afro-American women in literature—Study and teaching. 3. Afro-Americans in literature—Study and teaching. I. Title. II. Series.
    PS3573.A425 Z73 2000
    813'.54—dc21
                                                                00-041822

"What the finger writes the soul can read."

—Alice Walker

Contents

■■■■■■■■■■■■■■■■■■■■■■■■■■■■■■■■■■■■

Alice Walker is one of the most intriguing and most brutally honest writers alive today. This chapter provides background information about Walker's life, including her activism during the 1960s civil rights movement.

Guidelines for having students write their own poems modeled after Alice Walker's "Did This Happen to Your Mother? Did Your Sister Throw Up a Lot" and "Never Offer Your Heart to Someone Who Eats Hearts." Student samples included.

Alice Walker makes powerful use of spoken language in her novel The Color Purple. *The chapter explores ways in which students can develop the reading skills they need to navigate this challenging text.*

Alice Walker has been both revered and reviled. This chapter offers reviews and critical analysis of her work from various viewpoints. Reading what others have said about a published author helps students to reconsider and refine their own responses.

Alice Walker sometimes seems to be a magnet for controversy. This chapter explores issues of censorship in the classroom and provides suggestions for teachers committed to supporting their students' right to read.

Additional sources of information about Alice Walker and her work.

The NCTE High School Literature Series

■ ■

Apart from Emily Dickinson, Langston Hughes, and Mark Twain, few writers stand out as individuals in students' minds. Why should they? Teenagers seldom come across actual books of poetry or collections of stories by a single author. Even avid readers who have devoured every word of J. R. R. Tolkien's trilogy and all six of Douglas Adams's *Hitchhiker's Guide to the Galaxy* books, and who can recognize a page of Stephen King in a heartbeat, rarely have the same sense of recognition or love for a poet or short-story writer.

The reason has partly to do with instruction. More often than not, teachers serve students a smorgasbord of poems and stories, hoping that one will pique their appetite for more. Rather than developing a deep knowledge of a particular writer's work, students emerge with the vague sense that some poems and stories are "pretty cool" while others are "boring." This is not the kind of experience that makes for a lifelong love of the genre.

Textbook anthologies promote this topsoil approach to teaching poetry by scattering various poems, most often quite short and "multicultural," throughout their tomes, using verse to provide visual relief for the reader between longer prose excerpts. But poetry does not belong in a sidebar. And a few poems by Native Americans do not create a diverse collection of voices. What can offer balance to a traditional curriculum is the in-depth study of contemporary poets. When students read a collection of poems or stories by one author, written over many years and in a variety of moods and historical moments, they begin to determine for themselves what is unique about a writer, what makes him or her worthy of the exalted title, "artist."

As a classroom teacher working in a public urban high school, I know first hand the challenges involved in teaching literature to today's students. I know, too, that without powerful stories and poems to engage them, many will never acquire the literacy skills taxpayers and politicians praise so highly.

One-third of the students at Santa Monica High School are English-language learners. There are over twenty different languages spoken on campus. Our student body includes children who live in million-dollar homes and others who reside in homeless shelters. Diversity isn't something we work to achieve. What we work on is harmony.

Reading and writing poetry helps us to find the notes we share. My students have loved the literature in this series. I think yours will, too.

CAROL JAGO
Santa Monica High School
Santa Monica, California

Introduction

"Living by the Word"

Even a cursory glance at the chronology of Alice Walker's life is sure to leave a reader amazed. How could any writer be this productive, this prolific? Is there a genre Walker hasn't explored? Does she ever rest? Explaining her commitment to work, Walker wrote in her journal about a dream she once had of a two-headed woman.

> *April 17, 1984*
> The universe sends me fabulous dreams! Early this morning I dreamed of a two-headed woman. Literally. A wise woman. Who was giving advice to people. . . .
> I asked whether the world would survive, and she said, No; and her expression seemed to say, The way it is going there's no need for it to. When I asked her what I/we could/should do, she took up her walking stick and walked expressively and purposefully across the room. Dipping a bit from side to side.
> She said: Live by the Word and keep walking. (*Living by the Word* 1–2)

Teenagers often become discouraged by the global mess they feel they have inherited. Like Walker, they too wonder what it is that they could or should do. A few cynics take their cue from the dragon in John Gardner's *Grendel* and decide to find gold and sit on it. Idealists declare their commitment to ending world hunger or to curing cancer. Every one of my students wants to be happy. But how is genuine happiness possible in a world where so many seem doomed to suffer? I can think of no better answer than what the two-headed woman offered Alice Walker: "Live by the Word and keep walking."

Before they can live by the word, however, students must understand the power of the word to shape lives—both their own and other people's. Students need to learn about the glorious nuances in language and how words can be instruments of power. It is to this end that I teach Alice Walker's fiction, poetry, and essays. I know of no more intrepid explorer, no better model for constructing a life guided by principle and commitment to doing the right thing. Is Walker always right? I think she would be the first to say that we are all works-in-progress. As new learning and new experiences come our way, thoughtful individuals will and should change their minds.

Alice Walker is a national treasure. She is also one of the most interesting individuals alive today. Reviled almost as often as she is praised, Walker remains a champion for the right of every individual to self-determination. Students can learn a great deal from reading about how she has endeavored to live by the word. The classroom stories that follow demonstrate how students draw strength from the way Walker—often in the midst of opposition—has kept walking.

1 Where Life and Art Intersect

■ ■

Born into a sharecropping family in Georgia, Alice Walker is one of the best-known African American writers alive today. "As I remember it," Walker has said, "we were really not allowed to be discouraged. Discouragement couldn't hold out against my mother's faith." Empowered by her mother's faith, Walker dedicated her life to exploring—through both her writing and her activism—the lives of black women.

Childhood

The youngest of eight children, Alice Walker was a precocious child. Her mother enrolled her in first grade at the age of four, and Walker demonstrated from the very start a love for reading and a flair for writing. Realizing that her rambunctious older brothers were likely to find and destroy anything she committed to paper, the fledgling author composed poems in her head. This early training in creation influences her habits to this day. Walker has said that she plots her novels in visions that fill her head for a long period of time and then transfers them almost word perfect to a yellow pad. "When I'm ready to put it on paper that's pretty much the way it will be" (Whitaker 90).

Two of these rambunctious brothers almost blinded her. The children had been playing cowboys and Indians when a BB from one of the brothers' guns hit Walker in the eye. In "Beauty: When the Other Dancer Is the Self," Walker recounts the incident:

> I am eight years old and a tomboy. I have a cowboy hat, cow-
> boy boots, checkered shirt and pants, all red. My playmates
> are my brothers, two and four years older than I. Their colors
> are black and green, the only difference in the way we are
> dressed. . . . We chase each other for hours rustling cattle, be-
> ing outlaws, delivering damsels from distress. Then my par-
> ents decide to buy my brothers guns. These are not "real" guns.
> They shoot "BBs." Copper pellets my brothers say will kill birds.
> Because I am a girl, I do not get a gun. Instantly I am relegated
> to the position of Indian. Now there appears a great distance
> between us. (*In Search* 363)

The boys begged Walker not to tell their parents what had hap-
pened, and as a result a week went by before she saw a doctor.
His words would haunt Walker for years, "Eyes are sympathetic.
If one is blind, the other will likely become blind too."

Mining this experience for meaning—something at which she
is a master—Walker describes how the fear that she might lose
her sight has caused her to dash about the world hungrily, even
desperately, storing up visual images. In her poem "I Said to Poetry," the speaker, fed up with writing, holds a grudging conversation with her muse. In an effort to get the reluctant writer to
take up her pen once more, the muse reminds her, "You remember / the desert, and how glad you were / that you have an eye / to
see it with?" (*Her Blue Body* 353).

Adolescence

Along with the fear of losing her sight, the accident left Walker
feeling disfigured. Scar tissue had formed over the damaged eye,
and, with typical childhood brutality, classmates tormented her.
The confident little girl who once loved to perform suddenly became withdrawn and shy. Walker turned to books.

I am twelve. When relatives come to visit I hide in my room. My cousin Brenda, just my age, whose father works in the post office and whose mother is a nurse, comes to find me. "Hello," she says. And then she asks, looking at my recent school picture which I did not want taken, and on which the "glob," as I think of it, is clearly visible, "You still can't see out of that eye?"

"No," I say, and flop back on the bed over my book.

That night, as I do almost every night, I abuse my eye. I rant and rave at it, in front of the mirror. I plead with it to clear up before morning. I tell it I hate and despise it. I do not pray for sight. I pray for beauty. (*In Search* 366)

Over time Walker came to terms with the "glob." Though the scar tissue was eventually removed through surgery, the themes of vulnerability, inner versus outer beauty, and a celebration of the natural world continue to inspire Alice Walker's writing to this day.

College

Ironically, the accident that caused Walker to lose the sight of an eye, helped open the door for her to college, with support from the Georgia Department of Rehabilitation. The department offered financial assistance to physically challenged students. Alice received free textbooks and half her college tuition. Eager to enroll such a promising student, Spelman College presented her with an academic scholarship for the other half. The women in Walker's church raised another seventy-five dollars, and Alice was on her way.

It was at Spelman that Alice became involved in political activism. In 1962, she picketed the White House over the Cuban Missile Crisis and during the summer that followed her freshman year was chosen to attend the World Youth Peace Festival in Helsinki. Returning to Atlanta, Walker became involved in civil rights demonstrations organized by the Student Nonviolent Co-ordinating Committee (SNCC). These were heady days for a bright young woman keen to know the world and to fight for social justice. The following summer, Walker participated in the March on Washington for Jobs and Freedom. It was there that she heard Martin Luther King deliver the "I Have a Dream" speech.

After her sophomore year, Walker began to feel constrained at Spelman, an all-black college whose student body was made up of mostly middle and upper middle-class African American young women. Another scholarship opportunity allowed Walker to transfer to Sarah Lawrence College in Bronxville, New York, where she felt that she had more intellectual freedom as well as more support for her writing. In this new environment, she was one of only six African American students in the entire college.

It was at Sarah Lawrence that Walker began to write poetry in earnest. Every morning she took the poems she had written the day before and slid them under the door of her teacher, the extraordinary poet, Muriel Rukeyser. Rukeyser was impressed and showed the poems to her agent. Was it chance or the goddess of poetry that placed these two in such close proximity? I like to think that they were drawn to each other. Through Rukeyser's intervention, the collection *Once,* which includes many poems describing Walker's experiences during the civil rights movement ("Once," "Chic Freedom's Reflection," "Hymn"), was published by Harcourt Brace Jovanovich.

The Civil Rights Movement

After graduation, Walker fell in love with a white civil rights lawyer, Mel Leventhal, and moved with him to Mississippi. This act, in itself, was a form of protest because the state had passed a law forbidding interracial couples from living together. Though the law was declared unconstitutional by the United States Supreme Court, Walker and Leventhal lived in fear of reprisals from angry neighbors. Within this climate of racial tension, Walker continued to write, and her very first published essay, "The Civil Rights Movement: What Good Was It?" won first prize in the *American Scholar* contest. Walker also wanted to write about the Southern black women she was getting to know and coming to love. In a letter to a friend, Walker wrote that she would be staying in Mississippi for a while because "the stories are knee-deep" (*In Search* 224). In 1969, Walker gave birth to her daughter, Rebecca, and to her first novel, *The Third Life of Grange Copeland*.

Knee-Deep in Stories

To begin a series of lessons on Alice Walker's short story collection *In Love and Trouble: Stories of Black Women,* I took my cue from the author, asking my class of tenth graders to think about a time when they felt they were "knee-deep in stories."

RONNIE: Anybody want to come with me to my grandpa's tonight? You'll be knee-deep in something alright. Sometimes I feel like he's stuffing my head with stories about the good old days.

SALIMA: He probably just wants you to know what it was like back then or to know something about him. My grandmother is always telling me stories about how it was in Iran before our family had to leave. I don't remember any of what happened, so I guess it's her way of reminding me of where I come from.

Ms. JAGO: How do you feel when she's telling these stories?

SALIMA: A lot of times I'm just thinking about the homework I should be doing but sometimes the stories are pretty good. I like when she talks about what my dad was like as a little boy.

PEDRO: Yeh, those are good ones because then you can use them when your dad gets mad about you doing something wrong. But the stories I really like are the ones I hear when nobody thinks I'm listening. All the adults will just be sitting around late and they forget I'm still in the room and they just talk and talk and talk.

MS. JAGO: I think that's the kind of listening Alice Walker did when she was working among working-class black women in Mississippi. She was hired to teach African American history, but the students came from such diverse educational back-grounds that Walker wasn't sure where to begin. She decided to have the women begin by telling their own histories. These true stories were the seeds for Walker's short-story collection *In Love and Trouble*.

The Stories

Divide the class into five groups of students and give each group copies of one story from *In Love and Trouble*:

"Roselily"

This story juxtaposes the traditional lines from a marriage cer-emony with the internal monologue of a young woman, already the mother of four, who, in hopes of a better life, is getting mar-ried and moving to the North.

"Everyday Use"

The narrator is the mother of two daughters, one an outspoken, educated, modern young woman; the other, a reclusive home-body who as a child was injured badly in a fire. When Dee comes to visit and claims the family quilts for her own, the mother must choose between Dee's desire for the quilts as valuable heirlooms and pieces of art and Maggie's "everyday use" for them. This story is widely recognized as one of Walker's very best. It appears in the *Norton Anthology of African American Literature.*

"The Welcome Table"

In this beautifully simple story, Walker writes about an elderly black woman who is thrown out of a white church where she has come to pray. Walking away from the church, she meets Jesus on the road. Much is said in this story in very few words. If one of your groups of students is made up of slow readers, this is the ideal choice for them.

"Strong Horse Tea"

In this heartbreaking story of a young woman with a sick child, the mother does not want to resort to home remedies to cure her baby. Having asked the white mailman to bring the white doctor, she waits. To no one's surprise but her own, only her neighbor, an old woman with magic leaves around her neck, comes to her aid.

"To Hell with Dying"

Based on a real person in Alice Walker's life, Mr. Sweet—a diabetic, alcoholic, guitar player—is periodically brought back from the brink of death by the children who love him. This was Walker's first published short story. Muriel Rukeyser sent it to Langston Hughes who published it in *Best Short Stories by Negro Writers.* In an essay titled "The Old Artist," Walker writes:

> When I met Langston Hughes I was amazed. He was another Mr. Sweet? Aging and battered, full of pain, but writing poetry, and laughing, too, and always making other people feel better.

> It was as if my love for one great old man down in the poor and
> beautiful and simple South had magically, in the new world of
> college and literature and poets and publishing and New York,
> led me to another. (*Living by the Word* 40)

In 1988, the story "To Hell with Dying" was published as a
children's picture book.

The Assignment

Each student group is responsible for presenting its story to the
class in a manner that would make others interested in reading it.
In the presentation students should be warned not to give away
details that might spoil someone else's reading of the story but to
offer enough information to pique a reader's interest. Each student is also responsible for turning in a reading log containing
five to seven quotations from the story with accompanying re-
flections based on these quotes. Following the group presenta-
tions, students choose a second Alice Walker story to read. As a
culminating activity, students write a short essay exploring their
responses to Walker's short fiction.

A Metacognitive Moment

I believe it is important to let students know right from the start
where an assignment is heading. Though some may feel a bit
overwhelmed when they hear how much work they are going to
be expected to do over the next few days, this feeling is counter-
balanced by the sense that each individual classroom activity is
leading to a larger goal. Too often, I watch instruction become
fragmented and see students dutifully performing a series of seem-
ingly unrelated tasks without any idea how one is linked to the
next. Reminding students at every step of the lesson's goal—in

this case, to understand and appreciate Alice Walker's short fiction—gives our work together a sense of wholeness. The following stories are collected in her anthology *In Love and Trouble*.

Sample Student Reading Logs

Ronnie Nunez
From "The Welcome Table"

QUOTATION: "Auntie, you know this is not your church" (83).

RESPONSE: This is ironic because there is not supposed to be this kind of discrimination in the house of God. How could it not be the old lady's church? It shows how though the white people are pretending to be polite they are really discriminating against her for being black and poor.

Kara Greenspan
From "Everyday Use"

QUOTATION: "You just don't understand," she said, as Maggie and I came out to the car.
"What don't I understand?" I wanted to know.
"Your heritage," she said. And then she turned to Maggie, kissed her, and said, "You ought to try to make something of yourself, too, Maggie. It's really a new day for us. But from the way you and Mama still live you'd never know it" (59).

RESPONSE: I think what's happening here is that the author is showing how it's actually Dee who doesn't have a clue about what heritage really means. She's got her head all stuck up in the clouds and doesn't see what special people her mom and sister really are. If something doesn't fit in a picture frame or on the pages of a book, she can't see it. Smart as she is, she doesn't really understand much.

Salima Ladak
From "Strong Horse Tea"

QUOTATION: ". . . the frail breathing had stopped with the thunder, not to come again" (97).

RESPONSE: At first I didn't get it that this meant the baby had died but now I see that it does (Joe helped me with that). I think it's really sad because the mother will do anything to make her baby well again, but nothing can save him. I'm not sure I like stories that have endings like this one. Too depressing. That mailman should have told the doctor to come and help.

The Essay

After students have read two or three stories from *In Love and Trouble,* I ask them to formulate their ideas into an essay. I think student essayists should work in the style of Michel de Montaigne. Fed up with sixteenth-century discourse, Montaigne experimented with a new form of personal writing. He knew that what he was creating fit no traditional category, so he simply called what he produced *essays*—meaning attempts, or trials, or experiments. I want my students' essays to be experiments in thinking.

In his introduction to *The Norton Book of Personal Essays,* Joseph Epstein describes the essay as a form of discovery.

I sometimes make notes recalling anecdotes, facts, oddities of one kind or another that I wish to include in an essay, but where precisely in the essay they will be used I cannot say in advance. As for a previous design or ultimate goal for my essays, before I write them I have neither. The personal essay is, in my experience, a form of discovery. What one discovers in writing such essays is where one stands on complex issues, problems, questions, subjects. In writing the essay, one tests one's feelings, instincts, thoughts in the crucible of composition. (15)

I love that phrase: "the crucible of composition." Clearly, student writers need more guidance and structure than an accomplished essayist such as Epstein; I fear, however, that if we nail students to an artificial structure—the five-paragraph essay, for example—they will never know the intellectual joy of discovering what they think as they write. I am not suggesting that we allow students to turn in a stream-of-consciousness composition. Good writing is always carefully crafted. The best writing, however, is also inspired.

Often, I have students construct their own focus questions for their essays. On other occasions I offer them prompts. In any case, I always provide students with choices. The following essay questions have resulted in interesting student essays about *In Love and Trouble*:

1. Alice Walker was inspired to write these fictional short stories by the true stories that were told to her by Southern black women. Explain how Walker's made-up stories honor the deeper truths of these women's lives.

2. What themes do these stories seem to have in common? In your opinion, what does Walker seem to be saying about the people whose lives she portrays in the collection? Does the author seem sympathetic or critical, detached or involved?

3. Why do you think Walker called this collection *In Love and Trouble?* Please be very specific in describing how individual characters

find themselves in love and in trouble and how they deal with the love and trouble.

Assessment

After months of deliberation and countless hours of consensus building, the English department at my high school has adopted a rubric for evaluating student essays. I offer it here not as an example of how things should be done but rather as a draft from which teachers at your school might work. Our goal was to move toward holding students to common expectations across teachers and across grade levels. This rubric borrows from many published rubrics that have gone before. It is not perfect but does reflect our best intentions. If you would like an electronic copy, the rubric can be found on our English department Web site at *http:// english.samohi.org/*.

Santa Monica High School English Department
Analytical Essay Scoring Guide, Grades 9–12

A **6** paper presents an insightful analysis of the text, elaborating with well-chosen examples and persuasive reasoning. It has mature development and style. The 6 paper shows that its writer can use a variety of sophisticated sentences effectively, observe the conventions of written English, and choose words aptly.

A **5** paper presents a thoughtful and well-organized analysis of the text, elaborating with appropriate examples and sensible reasoning. It may contain minor errors of fact or interpretation. A 5 paper typically has a less fluent and complex style than a 6, but does show that its writer can vary sentences effectively, observe the conventions of written English, and usually choose words aptly.

A **4** paper presents an adequate analysis of the text, elaborating with sufficient examples and acceptable reasoning. It may contain some errors of fact or interpretation. Just as these examples and this reasoning will ordinarily be less developed than those in 5 papers, so will the 4 paper's style be less effective. Nevertheless, a 4 paper shows that its writer can usually control sentences of reasonable variety, observe the conventions of written English, and choose words of sufficient precision.

A **3** paper demonstrates some understanding of the text and prompt, but relevant analysis is minimal or absent. It may substantially misread or oversimplify the text. The paper may rely on plot summary, inappropriate or insufficient evidence, or move directly from evidence to inference. Its prose is usually characterized by at least one of the following: frequently imprecise word choice; little sentence variety; occasional major errors in grammar and usage, or frequent minor errors.

A **2** paper has serious weaknesses, ordinarily of several kinds. It frequently presents a simplistic or incoherent response, one that may suggest a major misunderstanding of the text or the prompt. It lacks specific evidence. Its prose is usually characterized by at least one of the following: simplistic or inaccurate word choice; monotonous or fragmented sentence structure; many repeated errors in grammar and usage.

A **1** paper suggests severe difficulties in reading and writing conventional English. It may disregard the prompt's demands, or it may lack any appropriate pattern of structure or development. It may be inappropriately brief. It often has a pervasive pattern of errors in word choice, sentence structure, grammar, and usage.

Without a doubt, the most valuable outcome of producing this rubric was the series of intense conversations about student writing that creating it entailed.

Potential Minefields

It would be remiss of me not to warn you that certain Alice Walker stories have been criticized as inappropriate for teenager's eyes. When "Roselily" appeared on a California statewide assessment, it drew criticism from those who felt that the story's main character, an unmarried mother of four, was morally reprehensible. Squeamish readers may be upset by "Strong Horse Tea." Although horse urine is a well-known folk remedy, they find the thought of drinking such medicine revolting.

Some students may object to the fact that white people are often the "bad guys" in Walker's stories, for example, in "The Welcome Table," where the pious white worshipers eject the old black woman from their church. What is important when students voice this criticism of Walker's writing is to ask them to consider the context of the stories. Is she stereotyping white mailmen when she has this character in "Strong Horse Tea" ignore the mother's plea for a doctor, or is Walker depicting one particularly callous individual who is also white? Was such behavior on the part of whites acceptable in the South at the time the story takes place? Ask students if they have ever felt they were discriminated against simply for being a teenager. This question never fails to bring out all kinds of horror stories about treatment from store detectives in the mall or about being ticketed for rolling through a stop sign by local police. How might their interpretation of the story shift if they, like many of Walker's characters, lived in a society that took for granted their second-class status?

I will be discussing the issue of censorship and self-censorship in greater detail within the context of Walker's novel *The Color Purple*. Here, I offer a single caveat: read every story before you assign it. One reason some teachers cling to textbook anthologies is that they know the stories that appear have passed a publisher's scrutiny for offensive language or subject matter. Trust your own judgment and your knowledge of your students and what is right for them; do not let yourself be blindsided. No one who has survived a censorship challenge would choose to repeat the experience.

2 Writing from Models

Few students respond with anything but groans to the news that they will be studying poetry. I believe such reaction is because their experience of poetry has mostly been one of bafflement. The typical scenario goes something like this. Teacher tells students that they are going to study a wonderful poem by _____ (fill in the blank). Teacher then tells students a few things about the wonderful poet. Teacher reads a poem aloud while students follow along in their books. Students find the poem incomprehensible. Teacher asks questions about the poem. Students stare into space. Uneasy with the silence, teacher answers her own questions. (A worse-case scenario has the teacher handing out the questions for students to answer "in complete sentences" for homework.) It isn't that students hate the genre. It's just that they have never yet met a poem they liked.

Inviting Students to Find a Poem They Like

A few years ago I decided to try to find an alternative to this deadly technique. Checking out all the individual volumes of poetry in our school library and then spreading them around the classroom, I asked students to find a poem that spoke to them and that they would like to share with the rest of us. I warned students some of the poems they might stumble upon would probably be rated R. I urged them to use good judgment. If a particular poem offended them, they should simply turn the page or pick up a different book. There was something for everyone's taste here.

   Since the task didn't seem too onerous, students readily complied. Browsing through the books, they tasted, rejected, picked up another volume, leaned across the aisle to show a friend what they had found, laughed, and generally carried on like kids in a candy store. No one seemed to have difficulty finding a poem to like. But then questions began floating to the front of the room. "Can we bring a poem from home?" "Is it OK to choose something we've written?" "What if the poem uses bad language?" "How long does it have to be?" "How long can it be?" "Can I read more than one?" Instead of answering their questions, I posed another, "What should be our criteria for choosing a poem to share?" Together we agreed on the following criteria:

   Poems to be shared should

- be able to be read in less than 3 minutes.
- be easy for listeners to understand.
- be something the chooser likes very much.
- use language appropriate for a school setting.
- cause listeners to think.
- cause listeners to want to hear the poem again or to read it for themselves.

This discussion seemed to answer their questions and help them make good choices. Employing this strategy for beginning a unit on poetry over the years, I began to notice a trend. Again and again students chose Alice Walker poems to share. Her books began to fall open to their favorite poems, for example, this poem from *Good Night, Willie Lee, I'll See You in the Morning*:

Did This Happen to Your Mother?
Did Your Sister Throw Up a Lot?
Alice Walker

I love a man who is not worth
my love.
Did this happen to your mother?
Did your grandmother wake up
for no good reason
in the middle of the night?

I thought love could be controlled.
It cannot.
Only behavior can be controlled.
By biting your tongue purple
rather than speak.
Mauling your lips.
Obliterating his number
too thoroughly
to be able to phone.

Love has made me sick.

Did your sister throw up a lot?
Did your cousin complain
of a painful knot
in her back?
Did your aunt always
seem to have something else
troubling her mind?

I thought love would adapt itself
to my needs.
But needs grow too fast;
they come up like weeds.
Through cracks in the conversation.
Through silences in the dark.
Through everything you thought was concrete.

Such needful love has to be chopped out
or forced to wilt back,
poisoned by disapproval
from its own soil.

This is bad news, for the conservationist.

My hand shakes before this killing.
My stomach sits jumpy in my chest.
My chest is the Grand Canyon
sprawled empty
over the world.

Whoever he is, he is not worth all this.

And I will never
unclench my teeth long enough
to tell him so. (2–3)

Using the Poems Students Like
as a Springboard for Instruction

If so many students felt this poem was powerful, it seemed fool-
ish for me to leave it to chance that they would find it on their
own. I began to incorporate Walker's poem into my lesson plans.
Writing only its title on the board, I asked students why they
thought Alice Walker might have called her poem "Did This Happen to Your Mother? Did Your Sister Throw Up a Lot?" Students
immediately recognized how effectively these questions capture
a reader's attention.

GUILLERMO: It's weird.

JAMIE: Yeah, it makes you want to find out if these are real questions or what.

MS. JAGO: So what do you think the poem is going to be about?

GUILLERMO: It reminds me of a movie I saw about a girl with bulimia. Maybe the poem is going to be about that.

SALIMA: I don't think so, Guillermo. I think she's being ironic or sarcastic or something like that. It seems too quirky to be realistic.

JAMIE: I'm not sure about quirky. I think it's going to be sad.

MS. JAGO: Why sad?

JAMIE: Well, I never saw anyone happy about throwing up.

MS. JAGO: Good point. Let's read and find out.

Louise Rosenblatt and Reader-Response Theory

What I hope to accomplish by this pre-reading activity is to move students from a passive to an active state. Background information about Alice Walker can wait. So can my lecture on free verse. What is important here is to lay the groundwork for genuine literary response. According to Louise Rosenblatt, good readers, active readers, conduct a transaction with the text. The reader creates meaning from the words on the page while the text causes the reader to reexamine what he or she knows. The text and the reader interact. By asking students to reflect on the title of a poem before they ever see the text, I hope to suggest that they are going to have to do some work here as a reader.

What is so powerful about Rosenblatt's insight into literature study is the way she situates the study of literature at the center of every child's life. It is not only the college-bound or future English teachers who need the nourishment that literature can provide, but also all students. She explains, "literature makes comprehensible the myriad ways in which human beings meet the infinite possibilities that life offers. The reader seeks to participate in another's vision—to reap knowledge of the world, to fathom the resources of the human spirit, to gain insights that will make his own life more comprehensible" (7). I cannot help but think that it was my students' unconscious recognition of Rosenblatt's insight that caused them to choose Alice Walker's poems year after year as their favorites. Walker was raising the same questions that they were asking themselves.

Metacognitive Moment Regarding
Cold Readings by Students

Having students read aloud a poem they have never seen before is often a painful experience for both reader and audience. A better idea is for you to practice reading the poem a few times and then read it to students. Voicing a poet's rhythms and language is difficult enough when you understand the poem's meaning. Trying to do so without this understanding is folly.

Responding on Paper

After reading "Did This Happen to Your Mother? Did Your Sister Throw Up a Lot?" to the class, I asked students to jot down their impressions of the poem. This simple task requires students to do some thinking on their own, uninfluenced by anyone else's interpretation. It also allows me to call on anyone in the class to share, though not necessarily to read, their response. I tell students that I want them to write nonstop for seven to nine minutes. If they run out of things to write, I suggest they return to the poem and copy a line that strikes them. This exercise usually gets them going again.

Joy Gallardo, an extraordinarily beautiful sixteen-year-old who misses an extraordinary number of school days every week, wrote:

The first line, "I love a man who is not worth my love" is such a good line. I've been in love with a man who wasn't worth my love simply because he was a jerk. He was very attractive but just couldn't control his mouth. He would hold me one second then call me a child the next. I mean if anyone had PMS, it sure wasn't me most of the time. His emotions would swing up and down. He would be laughing and smiling at me and then suddenly crying on my shoulder because he thought I didn't love him. I know what I should have done, which is break it off — but I didn't. I held on to him as long as I could until there wasn't any love left between us anymore. We have both grown quite a bit since then but never have thought about getting back together. Love is crazy.

While Joy's response is hardly literary analysis, it clearly demonstrates Rosenblatt's observation that readers turn to literature for insights that will make their own lives more comprehensible. Walker's poem reminded Joy of an experience when she loved a man who in her opinion was not "worthy of her love." Walker's solution, to "chop out" such "needful love" or to pull it out like a weed, felt right to her and to many others in the class. Elly Levin wrote about an ex-boyfriend who "laughed when I cried and I cried harder when he laughed." Pedro Reis wrote about a former girlfriend whose phone number he couldn't erase from his mind.

Imagery

As our discussion of the poem developed, student after student, both male and female, shared stories about how they or someone they knew had been mistreated in love. I asked them to reread the poem looking for the imagery Walker employed to describe this dysfunctional relationship. They pointed to "weeds," "concrete," and "poison" as well as verbs such as "biting," "vomiting," "chopping," and "killing." We talked about how imagery and diction creates the poem's tone.

ERIKA: The image I liked best was when she said "my chest is the Grand Canyon / sprawled empty / over the world." That's how you feel when someone you love walks out of your life, like there is so much space inside of you that can never be filled again.

BEN: It is great. And look how right in the next line she repeats what she said in the first line. The guy's not worth it.

ERIKA: But she can't stop thinking about him. I think that's why she wrote this poem.

JOY: Yeah, kind of like that song in *South Pacific* "I'm Gonna Wash That Man Right Outa My Hair." (Three girls from last year's musical cast burst into song.)

(Once order is restored, we continue.)

JOY: Sorry, Erika. I really agree with you. Alice Walker was probably trying to get over some guy. Love was making her sick.

Writing from Models

Knowing that these students had much more to say on this subject, I asked them as a homework assignment to write a poem modeled after Alice Walker's about a time when love made them sick. Along with offering them additional space to explore their response to this poem, I also felt that borrowing Walker's poetic structures would expand their own repertoire of poetic expression. Maybe I'm prejudiced, but I think Erika's poem is every bit as powerful as the original. At the same time, I have no doubt that Erika would never have written this poem without Walker's influence. It is untitled.

Untitled

I once loved a man with no name.
He had many names.
He had any name.
Have you ever done that?
Have you ever pushed yourself up the Invisible Man's sleeve
Looking for a warm place to hide?
Have you taken a carriage ride through Central Park?
And oh how the
frozen
vacant
winter
air
could mold beside you a million faces,
Cary Grant's smile,
Hercules' biceps,
Confucius' know-how.

He was right there!
He sat next to me whenever I wanted.

And you know how that swirl of loneliness looks.
It always mounts to a singular peak.
Did you drink from a half empty glass a lot?

That's not how it's supposed to be.

Desire is seasonal.
We pick its apples when they are red and ripe,
And bite all the way into the crisp white juices.
It dribbles on our chins.
It's messy.
It's supposed to be messy.

The same goes for that wretched snake,
Lust.

But apples rot.
After a couple bites they don't taste so good.
Then that white meat turns brown
and soft.
All the apples I buy rot.
I guess I leave them in the fruit basket too long.
I need to stay out of the produce section.
I won't waste my time anymore,
and I won't waste yours either.

You aren't the Invisible Man
with the
      warm
           safe
                sleeve.

—Erika Herman

Erika is very serious about her poetry and hopes to become a writer some day. When she read this to the class, students burst into spontaneous applause and then began discussing Erika's poem with the same intensity they had shown for Alice Walker's. It is this kind of connection between reading and writing, between appreciating literature and creating literature, that I try to foster. When it happens, it is magical.

When I asked if anyone else wanted to share their poems, students were reluctant. Erika's was a hard act to follow. Scanning the room for eyes that were tempted by my invitation, I cajoled Megan into reading her poem:

Were You a Good Girl before That Bad Boy Hurt You?

Were you a good girl before that bad boy hurt you?
I used to think that falling in love was easy.
I was wrong.

Did you like watching your love stab your heart with a knife?
Do you stab hearts now?
Good girls are no more.

Is your mother a bad girl?
Is your sister?
I was a good girl once
Until that bad boy paralyzed me.

My heart is gone now
Taken from me by that bad boy.
Now all I have left are pieces of hearts
Taken from all the good boys
I turned bad.

—Megan Torres

I am always amazed by how well students are able to borrow a writer's voice. The drop dead certainty of Megan's third line, "I was wrong" comes directly from Walker's poem though those particular words appear nowhere in the text.

Symbolism

We were clearly on a roll. Thinking to capitalize on students' interest in Alice Walker's subject matter and style, I handed out copies of "Never Offer Your Heart to Someone Who Eats Hearts." Along with "Did This Happen to Your Mother? Did Your Sister Throw Up a Lot?" this poem was first published in Walker's collection *Good Night, Willie Lee.*

Never Offer Your Heart
to Someone Who Eats Hearts
Alice Walker

Never offer your heart
to someone who eats hearts
who finds heartmeat
delicious
but not rare
who sucks the juices
drop by drop
and bloody-chinned
grins
like a God.

Never offer your heart
to a heart gravy lover.
Your stewed, overseasoned
heart consumed
he will sop up your grief
with bread
and send it shuttling
from side to side
in his mouth
like bubblegum.

If you find yourself
in love
with a person
who eats hearts
these things
you must do:

Freeze your heart
immediately.
Let him—next time
he examines your chest—
find your heart cold
flinty and unappetizing.

Refrain from kissing
lest he in revenge
dampen the spark
in your soul.

Now,
sail away to Africa
where holy women
await you
on the shore—
long having practiced the art
of replacing hearts
with God
and Song. (6–7)

Most students' initial response to the poem was "Gross!" But once we got past this visceral reaction (though I certainly intended to come back to it to illustrate Walker's sensual word choice), the most natural place to begin talking about the poem was with her use of the heart as a symbol. Students often struggle with symbolism. While they can learn to parrot back to you the symbolism of the road in Robert Frost's "The Road Not Taken" or the mockingbird in Harper Lee's novel, when it comes to thinking for themselves about how an object, person, or situation works as a symbol, students are often lost. The teacherly question, "Explain the symbolism in Wordsworth's 'I wandered lonely as a cloud,'" frustrates students because they feel powerless to figure out what things mean. Teachers always seem to have better answers.

One way to help students understand how symbols work is to ask them to think about private symbols. A particular bus stop may be a symbol for fear because it was the spot where a strange man once accosted them. They might have saved a movie stub from the night of their first kiss. The memento is a symbol for the experience. Car keys symbolize growing independence. Piercing a belly button may be a symbol of rebellion against parental control.

Literary symbols work in much the same way. They can be traditional, as in Alice Walker's use of a heart to symbolize love, or they can be intrinsic to the work, revealing themselves only gradually through repetition. Unlike other figures of speech such as a simile or metaphor, a symbol is often difficult to talk about. Much is left up to interpretation, particularly as a symbol may well affect one reader quite differently from the way it affects another. Many students mistakenly believe that symbols are planted in a poem like carrots, and that their job as careful readers is to pull them out for counting and identification. Unfortunately, it is possible that our own manner of questioning students encourages such a view.

Sven Birkerts compares a symbol to a force field, "sending out waves of suggestion that penetrate many layers of the work and add to its meaning. They are not to be extracted so much as probed and questioned. . . . Symbols tend to point outward; they do not so much mean as suggest" (125).

I asked students to reread the poem and consider what the heart suggests.

MEGAN: Everybody knows that hearts symbolize love, but in this poem the writer makes you think about what it means when someone is a heart-eater. This is weird because it reminds me of that poem I just wrote.

MS. JAGO: Were you thinking about the heart as a symbol when you wrote your poem?

MEGAN: Heck, no. It just seemed like a good way to explain what I wanted to say about this really abusive relationship I was once in.

BEN: Do you think all writers do that, just write, and then leave it to teachers to figure out the symbolism?

MS. JAGO: How about we say "readers" instead of teachers. English teachers don't have a monopoly on symbol identification, you know.

BEN: Sure. Right. But what about my question? Do poets plan what symbols they are going to use or does it just happen accidentally?

ERIKA: I think it happens both ways. Sometimes I start with a symbol, like that Invisible Man in my poem. Sometimes I write something and somebody else tells me what it means later.

MEGAN: So what does your Invisible Man symbolize?

ERIKA: That's not fair. Alice Walker doesn't have to answer questions about her poems. Besides, if I tell you then you'll think my answer is the only right one.

MEGAN: If Alice Walker were here I'd ask her, too. She probably would give me the same run-around, though. You poets always want to be all mysterious and vague.

This was exactly the discovery I had hoped students would come to. Looking for symbols in poetry can be a tricky business. Seldom does A simply equal B. The heart may symbolize love, but in Walker's poem it also suggests vulnerability as well as a wound. Many readers find her description of the heart as an edible organ grotesque. More than anything else, it is probably this that makes the poem unforgettable. Guillermo was so moved by Walker's poem that he went home and, borrowing heavily from her imagery and symbolism, wrote a poem that offers advice about protecting one's heart.

Never Give Your Heart to Someone Who Steps on Hearts

Never give your heart
To someone who steps on hearts
Someone who finds that she likes
The squishy feeling,
One who loves to stomp,
The kind who likes the look of
Heart chunks on her shoes.

Never give your heart
To women with stiletto heels
For your heart will quickly know
What ground beef feels like
As she steps and pivots
And grinds you into hell.

If you find yourself
In love
With a person who steps
On hearts,
Then follow these instructions:

Armor your heart with the toughest steel,
Let her find your heart
Is strong and unstompable.
Next, grab her by the feet
And tell her you'll cut them off
The next time she tries
To step on your heart.

If you have followed my words of advice,
Then your heart should be whole and footprintless.

—Guillermo Lopez

More than any quiz could ever show, this poem demonstrates Guillermo's deep understanding of Walker's poem. Do I need to ask him to explain her use of symbolism? Should I have him identify the line where Walker's poem turns? Must I ask him to define an extended metaphor? In my professional opinion, Guillermo has told me everything I need to know.

3 *The Color Purple*

What does it mean "to teach" a novel such as *The Color Purple*? As with any book, I know that I want students to read the book and then to think about what they have read; translating these two simple goals into classroom practice, however, is always a challenge. In teaching this novel, which admittedly is challenging, I need to complete several tasks in order to help students better understand the work. With this goal in mind, I

- address Walker's epistolary format for students unfamiliar with the form.

- encourage students to question the author and the text rather than relying on me to pose discussion questions.

- help students who say they can't understand the dialect.

- pace reading assignments so that slower readers aren't overwhelmed yet speedy readers aren't frustrated.

- check periodically to make sure that students are actually reading the book.

- deal with sexually explicit passages and graphic language (see Chapter 5).

- assess students in a manner that pushes them to think more deeply about Walker's story.

First, Do No Harm

As I read *The Color Purple*, I grew transfixed by the story. Years later, I can still picture with perfect clarity the couch where I sat and the evening I spent with the book.. I could not put the book down. I would like for students to have similarly intense reading experiences; however, too often it seems that everything about school and about "teaching" a book works against this goal. How can I provide a scaffold for readers who need help—particularly at the beginning of a novel—without sending students the message that they need me in order to understand what they are reading? How can I share my insights from the work without implying that these are the best insights to be garnered as well as the correct interpretation? How can I hold students accountable for their reading? I wish I could tell you that I have simple answers to these questions and that what follows is a foolproof method for teaching this or any other novel. It's not. What I can do, however, is offer a snapshot of how I teach a novel such as *The Color Purple* that I believe avoids ruining the book for kids.

I begin by asking students if they have ever written letters over a period of time to a friend or family member. The few who have done so often comment on how good it feels to be able to tell their side of the story knowing the reader can't check up on them. Students immediately see how similar such writing is to keeping a diary.

Ms. Jago: Why do you think someone might decide to write letters to God?

Kara: Well, maybe you'd write to God if you didn't have any friends or family, but I don't see why God instead of "Dear Diary."

PEDRO: Maybe the person is religious. I mean, if you believe that God cares about you but nobody else does, then it would make sense to write to God.

KARA: I guess.

ERIKA: It would be a lot like a diary, though, because if you're writing to God you're not exactly expecting a letter in return so it's writing for the sake of writing.

MS. JAGO: What do you mean when you say "writing for the sake of writing"?

JAMIE: It's like writing to yourself just to figure out what you're thinking. I used to keep a diary when I was little and it felt good to write about how much I hated my sister and to call her "The Spider" on paper without getting in trouble from my mom.

PEDRO: I would never write like that because I have lots of friends that I talk to all the time, but I could see how somebody might write just for nothing if they had no friends. You know sometimes you've just got to get something out and it doesn't matter what your friend who's listening says. It only matters that he's listening.

Pedro's comments served as a perfect context for opening our copies of *The Color Purple*. The story begins:

You better not never tell nobody but God. It'd kill your mammy.

Dear God,
I am fourteen years old. I am I have always been a good girl. Maybe you can give me a sign letting me know what is happening to me. (1)

Good-Enough Reading

One of the greatest challenges inexperienced readers face when beginning a novel is negotiating the first twenty pages. Many students give up and declare the book "boring" before they ever get a sense of the story or characters. One reason is that these students often aren't confident enough readers to trust that though things may seem confusing in the early pages, all will become clear if they forge ahead thoughtfully. Accomplished readers suspend their immediate need to know and move quickly through the opening of a novel. Instead of getting bogged down by details that don't seem to make sense, confident readers gather information about characters, setting, and circumstances—a bit like detectives on a case. Think about the first chapter of most science fiction novels. Often a reader can't even be sure of the main character's species let alone the rules of this fictional world.

As your eyes scan this line of print, a number of seconds have transpired. Just how many seconds largely depends on your familiarity with the vocabulary and with your deep knowledge of the kind of text in your hands. You are most likely able to skip lightly and quickly down this page because you understand how books like this work. When something untoward appears, something that doesn't make sense or seems out of context, you send your eyes back to check the strange information that has just been sent to your brain.

In a novel, particularly a complex one, such checking does not always clear up the problem right away. Writers of fiction often set out to puzzle their readers, confident that if you are intrigued enough by their story, you will keep turning the pages to find out more. In fact most authors covet the term "a page-turner" for their book jackets. Experienced readers of fiction engage in what Margaret Mackey from the University of Alberta calls "good-enough reading." She defines this as "the ability to strike a personal balance between the need for momentum and the need for accountability to the text" (430).

I was struck by this definition because I know that I often urge my students to do such good-enough reading, particularly for the first thirty pages or thirty minutes. What happens in this interval is that the reader proceeds with less than complete information. Sometimes the relationships among the characters seem to make no sense. Other times, the fictional world is so foreign to the reader that simply exploring the terrain requires a chapter or two. Experienced readers learn to forge ahead, confident that the writer won't lead them astray. Have they missed or misunderstood some important information? Most likely. But the absence of these details doesn't block the reader's forward progress. For the purposes of fiction, "good-enough" reading is a positive virtue. It keeps readers engaged and actively revising their understanding of the story as it evolves.

Getting Started: *The Color Purple*

I often have students read the first chapter of a novel in class. What I am trying to accomplish by this is to help them deal with the unfamiliar aspects of the book and begin to engage in the story before sending them off with a homework reading assignment. Introducing the novel by telling students about the characters or author never seems to work for me because it spoils the joy of discovery for some while others—those who I think most need help—typically tune out.

The Color Purple is not organized into chapters but rather as a series of letters. I ask students to flip through the novel so that they can see how this epistolary format continues throughout the book. This activity also allows reluctant readers to notice all the white space on the pages of Walker's text.

I then ask students to read for twenty minutes and to note where they have stopped (you might be surprised to discover how many students don't do this by habit). I have them take out a piece of paper and tell them we are going to write for fifteen minutes not summarizing or explaining what they have read but rather questioning the text. I suggest they begin with a question that is bothering them right now or that they are wondering about and to let this question lead to others. If possible explanations come to mind, they should write these down, too. I invite students to let their questions lead to answers that in turn lead to new questions. "How" and "Why" questions usually work best. About a minute before their time is up, I ask students to write a final sentence that begins with "I wonder . . ."

Yessica Mesias wrote:

I don't understand why the author wrote Mr.
instead of a name for this character. This is bugging me. I keep wanting to fill in the blanks. I guess I'll get used to this but right now it's really distracting. Why did she do this? Well maybe the author wants to say he's Mister Nobody or Mister X or a mystery man. Maybe she's saying that there is a lot the person writing these letters doesn't know. Even for a fourteen-year-old, Celie seems pretty clueless about what's going on in her own life. Pretty harsh life, though. I wonder if Celie will run away.

Cyyrill Yared wrote:

I guess the person writing these letters is talking about being pregnant and having babies but it seems crazy to me that she doesn't have any control over what is happening to her. When is this story taking place? Can't she go to some kind of social worker or something for help? Mr.   says she's dumb but her sister Nettie says she's not. Is she? I mean her grammar is bad and all that but she's always trying to figure out what's happening to her. I don't think Celie knows for sure herself if she's dumb or smart. I wonder why the author doesn't use quotation marks when people talk in the story.

Students enjoy doing this kind of freewriting. As we share our questions and tentative answers, I ask students to think about how the writing helped them think about what they were reading.

Ms. Jago: How did writing like this help your reading?

Jamie: It was weird. Sometimes as soon as I wrote a question, the answer popped in my head. I don't know if what I thought was right or anything, but it did kinda make sense.

Pedro: Yeah. That happened to me, too. I think maybe if you didn't make us write questions I never would have known what I didn't know and then just read on getting more and more confused. This way I at least have something to hang on to.

Cyyrill: But aren't we doing your job for you here, Mrs. Jago? I mean, aren't you paid to be asking the questions?

Ms. Jago: What do you think?

Jamie: I think if Mrs. Jago always asks the questions, then mine might never come up.

Pedro: And it's different, too. When you're answering a teacher's questions, you're always trying to guess what's on her mind. This is more like guessing what's on the author's mind.

Writing this kind of "question paper" also helps students begin to see that with a bit of thinking they often can discover answers to their own questions. By looking within themselves and then back at the text, students begin to develop one of the most valuable habits of good readers—questioning the text. Their repertoire of questions might include the following:

Based upon what I know of the world, does this character's actions make sense? If not, why not?

Did I miss something as I read or is there something in this fictional world that I don't yet understand?

What does the author's attitude toward these events seem to be? What is the author trying to make me feel here?

As long as the teacher remains the source of all correct answers, students remain convinced that challenging literature is a puzzle they can never master. The more practice they get in posing their own questions and positing tentative explanations, the more confident and competent they become as readers.

Getting through *The Color Purple:* Language

Some students may find Celie's language difficult to understand.

That's a real pretty dress you got on, he say to Nettie.
She say, Thank you.
Them shoes look just right.
She say, Thank you.
Your skin. Your hair. Your teefs. Everyday it something else to make miration over.

First she smile a little. Then she frown. Then she don't look no special way at all. She just stick close to me. She tell me, Your

skin. Your hair, Your teefs. He try to give her a compliment, she
pass it on to me. After while I git to feeling pretty cute. (18)

In order to convey an authentic sense of Celie's inner speech,
Walker abandons many of the conventions of spelling and punc-
tuation. I ask students to look at this passage and to think about
what Walker's choice of syntax and diction reveals about Celie.
After reading and talking about a few such passages aloud, students usually find they can negotiate Celie's sentences on their
own without stumbling.

I want to be careful about what I am recommending here.
Reading aloud is the most popular and arguably the most successful method for getting kids hooked on books. However, reading aloud should not become a substitute for independent reading.
The problem is that too often reading aloud has become the in-
structional method of choice for getting middle and high school
students through a text. Unless the purpose of the lesson is a
celebration of language or, in this case with *The Color Purple,* a
lesson on learning how to read the spoken word, students—not
their teachers—should be doing the reading.

Reading aloud is often employed in the classroom for many
of the wrong reasons: an insufficient number of copies of a book
to send home with students, students' poor reading skills, students' refusal to do homework. As a result, many teenagers are
doing very little reading. Only a few pairs of eyes follow along in
the text as the teacher reads aloud. The classroom may be quiet
and the lesson may seem productive. A principal passing by the
classroom door would think, "My, what a good teacher," but the
only person whose reading skill is improving is the teacher's.

In his 1987 Nobel Prize acceptance speech, Joseph Brodsky
explained, "In the history of our species, . . . the book is an

anthropological development, similar essentially to the invention of the wheel. Having emerged in order to give us some idea not so much of our origins as of what the Sapiens is capable of, a book constitutes a means of transportation through the space of experience, at the speed of turning a page" (5). The challenge for teachers is to help students operate this curious means of transportation and to get them turning those pages. English teachers agree that taking the textual trip through "the space of experience" is essential. What we struggle with is figuring out how to keep young readers moving.

Getting through *The Color Purple:* Pacing

Once the class has entered an author's fictional world, I like to give students a great deal of latitude in terms of how they pace their reading. Some will want to devour *The Color Purple* whole in a night. Others will prefer to stagger their reading over several weeks. Rather than assign a particular number of pages per night, I set a date when the novel is due and then help students figure out what they need to do to meet that deadline.

This help takes the form of an unscientific experiment wherein we calculate how long it will take each student to complete *The Color Purple.* I ask students to make themselves as comfortable as possible with the book in hand—no distractions, no interruptions. We then time ourselves for twenty minutes of reading during which students move through the text as quickly as they can while still attending to the meaning of what they read. Students record the page number on which they begin and the page number where they stop.

At the end of the twenty minutes, I put the following set of instructions on the board for their calculations:

Student's name:

Book title: *The Color Purple*

Starting page #: _____

Ending page #: _____

Number of pages read in 20 minutes:

Number of pages read in 20 minutes multiplied by 3:
(This gives students the number of pages in this particular book that they can read in an hour.)

Number of pages read in an hour divided by 60:
(This gives students the number of pages in this particular book that they can read in a minute.)

Total pages in the book:

Approximately how long will it take you to read *The Color Purple?*

To calculate this figure, students multiply the total number of pages in the book by their reading rate. For example, if a student reads half a page per minute and the book is three hundred pages long, it will take the student six hundred minutes, or ten hours, to complete the novel. Ideally, a high school student should be able to read a page a minute. Clearly a student's reading pace depends on the density of the print as well as on the complexity of the text, but aiming for a page a minute is a reasonable goal.

I then hand each student a calendar (for the next three weeks) and ask them to fill in the number of minutes a day that they plan to read in order to make the deadline. While planning ahead like this may seem the most natural thing in the world to compulsively organized teachers, it is often a foreign concept to students.

By helping students plan how to get from here to there, we help to keep them from failing. Knowing it will take them six hours to finish the novel, students also know that this will not be possible to accomplish on Thursday night if they are working until 10 p.m.

I hope that students will find themselves so caught up in Alice Walker's novel that all thought of pages to be read and deadlines to be met will disappear. Experience has taught me, however, that many students need structures to help them discipline themselves to the task of reading an entire novel.

Assessment: How Do You Know Students Have Done the Reading?

Every time classroom teachers ask simplistic questions about a piece of literature, they undermine students' confidence as readers. Take, for example, the following test item:

In Alice Walker's *The Color Purple,* the narrator has
  a. one brother
  b. one sister
  c. one brother and one sister
  d. no siblings

This is a dumb question. I suppose it could be defended if the teacher is simply trying to check to see whether students have done the reading, but I want to argue that posing such questions actually does harm. Dumb questions send students the message that the purpose of reading is to answer questions. If my goal is to foster the love of literature, it does not make sense to ask students to match "Nettie" with the description "Celie's beloved sister." I like to think that I would already know which students have not done the reading on the basis of their participation in class (or lack thereof). Punishing these kids doesn't actually solve the problem. Why waste valuable class time finding out what I already know?

Quizzes full of dumb questions also foster a competitive spirit in the classroom. Scores encourage students to label one another as "smarter-than-me" or "dumber-than-me," an attitude that can result in severely circumscribed classroom discussion. Consider such categorization from a student's point of view—it's hard to feel good about contributing to a discussion on Monday when you have just been handed a flaming red D from Friday's quiz.

Teachers contradict themselves when, in one breath, they tell students to say what they think or feel about a piece of literature, and in the next, ask them to fill in the name of the tribe in Africa with whom Nettie lived. Often, even the most astute readers find they can't remember this level of detail off the top of their heads. Does making grade distinctions between readers who can and can't recall plot details encourage students to read more thoughtfully? I think not. It takes confidence for students to share their interpretations with others. Ideally, every voice will have weight and substance and will add to the group's collective understanding of the text. For this to happen, however, students must respect one another's varied interpretations and regard one another as thinkers.

Seminar-Style Discussions

Hannah Arendt has observed, "For excellence, the presence of others is always required." Actors, musicians, athletes all know how their own performance is enhanced by the presence of an audience. But what about readers? Does this most solitary of acts also require company for excellence? Sometimes I think it does.

On the day I had set for students to have completed their reading of *The Color Purple,* I explained that instead of taking a test or writing an essay about the novel, we would hold a seminar. Since this was to take the place of a more formal assessment, everyone would be expected to speak up and participate. Students readily agreed. Whether they did so out of genuine enthusiasm for my idea or relief at not having to write a paper, I leave to your imagination.

The rules for these classroom seminars have been adapted from many sources and change with every group of students I teach. A few things remain constant:

- Desks are arranged in a circle.

- All speakers are to be heard with respect.

- Whenever appropriate, specific passages from the text should be referred to, even reread aloud. Nothing other than *The Color Purple* should be on their desks.

- No one need raise a hand. As I wasn't going to be asking the questions or calling on them, students would need to exercise courtesy taking turns speaking. If one person begins to monopolize the conversation, it is the responsibility of the group to call on one another for other opinions.

- It is up to the group to generate the discussion and in so doing to demonstrate their understanding of the novel. Moments of thoughtful silence can help the conversation move in a new direction.

- I may not enter into the discussion. In the final three minutes of class I will describe what I observed during the seminar and make suggestions for future seminars.

Jamie began. "The last section of *The Color Purple* where everybody comes together for the family reunion seemed just too perfect to be true. I mean what are the chances of everybody being in the same place and all getting along after everything that's happened?"

"I see what you mean," said Pedro, "But I really liked that that was the way the story ended. Celie had been through so much pain and those other characters like Sophia, too, that I really needed it to all work out for them."

Kara disagreed. "Life isn't going to be happy ever after for these people, Pedro. Look at the rules of the society they are living in. In some ways things are better because Celie's more confident now and has made her peace with her husband, but I'll bet there are going to be problems with these kids of hers from Africa."

Megan interrupted, "Yeah, imagine how people will treat Adam and Tashi with those scars on their faces."

"I think the scars are symbols for how they're different inside from everyone else at that reunion." Kara continued. "Celie may feel good today, but she's probably going to have her heart broken again."

The conversation continued in this vein for the next forty minutes. To anyone who delights in watching young people learn, the seminar was breathtaking. Students listened to one another, probed each other's observations, argued, asked serious questions, and pointed to the text. When it was over I could have kissed every one of them. Instead, I let them know that this was as good as the study of literature gets. All of the other activities we engage in along the way are simply preparation for this kind of exchange, for just this kind of conversation among readers about texts.

After class, Joy came up to let me know that they really should have had more time for the discussion. I often wonder if students are this blunt with all their teachers. Mine never seem to hesitate telling me what I should do better. Of course, Joy was right.

To View or Not to View: Steven Spielberg's Version of *The Color Purple*

Except under rare circumstances, I don't think English teachers should show students film versions of assigned novels. I realize that with forty-nine states adopting language arts standards with references to viewing, that this is a radical stance. I also want to go on record as believing that the study of film as genre is an important and lasting outcome of a liberal arts education. Instruction in viewing and film, however, should not occur in an English class. Our curriculum is already full.

Every moment in an English class is precious. By the time a teacher has taken attendance, made a few announcements, and tuned in the VCR, only about forty minutes of the period is left for the movie. This means that a feature such as Steven Spielberg's *The Color Purple* will take three class periods to show. If a teacher shows five movies in a school year—which given the number of excellent film adaptations of novels now available doesn't seem unreasonable—students will have lost fifteen days or three weeks of class time to "viewing." I do not believe this is a wise use of students' time. Too often when the lights go down and the TV monitor lights up, teenagers hit their internal relax button and shut down all critical faculties. Some pull out their calculators and start their math homework. A few put their heads down for a snooze. However the lesson has been framed, too many students consider a day watching a movie as a day off.

Despite my strong feelings about the danger of showing movies in English class, I believe that *The Color Purple* is an important movie for students to see. Rated PG-13, the Spielberg film can serve as a powerful vehicle for critical thinking and thoughtful viewing. Alice Walker worked closely with Steven Spielberg on the film and took part in many of his artistic decisions. As Walker said in an interview about the film, "We may miss our favorite part, but what is there will be its own gift. I hope people will be able to accept that in the spirit that it's given" (Price 1).

The 1985 movie unleashed a torrent of criticism from within the African American community. Walker was accused of hating black men and conspiring with white Hollywood to degrade the black family by portraying violence, incest, rape, and lesbianism. Forums were held throughout the country at which the film's themes were hotly debated, often by people so angry about what they had heard about *The Color Purple* that they refused to see it. Some demanded to know why a black man, such as Sidney Poitier, hadn't directed it. Others wanted to know why Walker and Spielberg focused on the failings of black men rather than their achievements. These are important questions for students to grapple with.

Alice Walker reacted to the backlash against the film first with pain, then numbness, and finally by letting go. In her book *The Same River Twice: Honoring the Difficult,* Walker reflects on this tumultuous time. "It was a rare critic who showed any compassion for, or even noted, the suffering of the women and children explored in the book, while I was called a liar for showing that black men sometimes perpetuate domestic violence. . . . Though *The Color Purple* is not what many wished, it is more than many hoped, or had seen on a movie screen before. It still moves me after all these years, as I relive the feeling of love that was palpable on the set" (123).

Alice Walker's favorite scenes from the movie include the parting of young Celie and her beloved sister, Nettie; the struggle of Nettie to defend herself against Mister's sexual advances; the tender kiss between Celie and Shug; Celie's discovery of letters from Nettie that Mister had hidden; and Shug's first song in the roadhouse. One way to seed a class discussion comparing the film and book is to have students engage in written conversations.

Comparing the Book and Film: Written Conversations

Before students arrive, I prepare a list pairing them with a partner. In order to build relationships within our classroom community, I purposely pair students who do not know each other well. After making adjustments for absentees and inserting my own name if necessary, we complete the following tasks:

- Think of a scene from the movie that we particularly liked. Write for five minutes about why this scene was so affecting, comparing it with how Walker portrayed the scene in her book.

- After five minutes, students exchange papers with their partners and begin writing back, responding to what they read.

- This process is repeated back and forth for as long as students seem focused on the task. As they become increasingly engaged, I often extend the time for writing. I urge them to include questions in their notes to one another, as queries offer respondents an immediate entry point—even if the answer is "Heck, I don't know, either!"

- When I feel students' hands are giving out from the nonstop writing, I tell them to sit down with their partner and continue the conversation.

What I particularly like about this activity is that every student must enter into the discussion. Often teenagers sit back and wait for the "talkers" in the class to do all the work, confident that as long as somebody is speaking, the teacher will leave them alone. I also like that, apart from collecting their papers so students know the assignment "counted," I don't need to correct their work. When you meet with one hundred and fifty students a day, it is not possible to read every student paper.

In a poem from *Good Night, Willie Lee,* Alice Walker writes about the completion of *The Color Purple:*

Now That the Book Is Finished
Alice Walker

Now that the book is finished,
now that I know my characters
will live,
I can love my child again.
She need sit no longer
at the back of my mind,
the lonely sucking of her thumb
a giant stopper in my throat. (20)

4 Taking a Critical Stance

Reading what others have said about a writer's work can help students refine and even reconsider their own responses. The problem with Alice Walker is that more has been written about her than almost any other contemporary writer. As a result, students researching Walker can become easily overwhelmed. What follows are excerpts from articles that deal with important aspects of Walker's literary contribution to American letters. These essays are offered as interpretations open for discussion, not definitive views.

Critics on Alice Walker

bell hooks

A feminist scholar-activist, poet, and social critic, hooks is known for her unflinching examination of American culture and for her deconstructive analyses of race and gender. Though students may find hooks's academic prose challenging to negotiate, her insights into the text may push them to new understandings.

Writing the Subject: Reading The Color Purple

The Color Purple broadens the scope of literary discourse, asserting its primacy in the realm of academic thought while simultaneously stirring the reflective consciousness of a mass audience. Unlike most novels by any writer it is read across race, class, gender, and cultural boundaries. It is truly a popular work—a book of the people—a work that has many different meanings for many different readers. Often the meanings are not interesting, contained as they are within a critical discourse that does not resist the urge to simplify, to overshadow, to make this work by a contemporary African-American writer mere sociological treatise on black life or radical feminist tract. To say even as some critics do that it is a modern day "slave narrative" or to simply place the work within the literary tradition of epistolary sentimental novels is also a way to contain, restrict, control. Categorizing in this way implies that the text neither demands nor challenges, rather, that it can be adequately and fully discussed within an accepted critical discourse, one that remains firmly within the boundaries of conservative academic aesthetic intentionality. While such discourse may illuminate aspects of the novel, it also obscures, suppresses, silences.

To critically approach *The Color Purple* from an oppositional perspective, it is useful to identify gaps—spaces between the text and conventional critical points of departure. That the novel's form is epistolary is most obvious, so apparent even that it is possible to overlook the fact that it begins not with a letter but with an opening statement, a threatening command—speaker unidentified. "You better not never tell nobody but God. It'd kill your mammy." Straightaway Celie's letter writing to God is placed in a context of domination; she is obeying orders. Her very first letter reveals that the secret that can be told to no one but God has to do with sexuality, with sexual morality, with a male parent's sexual abuse of a female child. In form and content the declared subject carries traces of the sentimental novel with its focus on female characters and most importantly the female as potential victim of exploitative male sexual desire, but serves only as a background for deviation, for subversion.

Source: bell hooks, "Writing the Subject: Reading *The Color Purple*," in *Alice Walker*, ed. Harold Bloom (New York: Chelsea House, 1989), 215–16.

■ ■ ■ ■ ■ ■ ■ ■ ■ ■ ■ ■ ■ ■ ■ ■

Maria V. Johnson

Maria V. Johnson is currently visiting on the faculty at Stanford University, where she is completing a manuscript on African American women writers and the blues tradition. You may want to play a few blues tunes for students before sharing this essay with them.

"You Just Can't Keep a Good Woman Down": Alice Walker Sings the Blues

Alice Walker has been profoundly influenced and inspired both by African American music and musicians and by writers whose work is grounded in music and in the expressive folk traditions of African Americans. Zora Neale Hurston's *Their Eyes Were Watching God* and the blues music of blues women like Bessie Smith rank among Walker's most significant musical/literary influences. In her words, "Music is the art I most envy . . . musicians (are) at one with their cultures and their historical subconscious. I am trying to arrive at that place where Black music already is; to arrive at that unself-conscious sense of collective oneness; that naturalness, that grace" (*In Search of Our Mothers' Gardens*, 259).

In "Nineteen Fifty-five" and *The Color Purple*, Walker

employs the character, language, structure, and perspective of the blues to celebrate the lives and works of blues women, to articulate the complexity of their struggles, and to expose and confront the oppressive forces facing Black women in America. In her portraits of blues women, Walker shows us the vitality, resiliency, creativity, and spirituality of African American women, illuminating the core aesthetic concepts which have been crucial to their survival in a society that has largely used and abused them for its own purposes. Indeed, in Walker's works, African American women performers and their performances symbolize vitality and aliveness, and the will and spirit not only to endure but potentially to flourish. The blues woman, whose song is true to her own experience and rooted in the values and beliefs of the community, empowers those who love her and effects change in those around her. Her outer struggles and inner conflicts reflect issues of oppression in society as they have been internalized within the community.

In addition to blues characters, Walker employs blues forms, themes, images, and linguistic techniques. Her forms—letters and diary entries—are like blues stanzas in their rich compactness and self-containedness; like blues pieces, her works take shape from the repetition and variation of these core units. Walker's focus on the complexities and many-sidedness of love and relationships repeats the subject of many blues songs.

Source: The full essay from which this excerpt was taken can be found at http://www.sistahspace.com/sistory/writers/walker/youjust.html.

Harold Bloom

Harold Bloom is Sterling Professor of the Humanities at Yale University and professor of English at New York University Graduate School. He is general editor of the Chelsea House Series, *Modern Critical Views*. Bloom contends that critics have idealized the interrelationships among women writers and among black women writers in particular.

A contemporary writer who calls herself "author and medium" is by no means idiosyncratic, and Alice Walker certainly seems to me a wholly representative writer of and for our current era. The success of *The Color Purple* is deserved; Walker's sensibility is very close to the Spirit of the Age. Rather than seek to analyze verse and fictional prose that is of a kind I am not yet competent to judge, or a speculative essay such as "In Search of Our Mothers' Gardens" which eludes me, I will center here upon Walker's meditations upon her acknowledged precursor, Zora Neale Hurston. "There is no book more important to me than this one," Walker wrote of Hurston's masterwork, *Their Eyes Were Watching God*. Perhaps the only literary enthusiasm I share with Walker is my own deep esteem for that admirable narrative.

The Color Purple's Celie indeed writes "herself into being in a language that imitates that idiom spoken by Janie and Hurston's black community generally." The authority of the male voice, and its sexism, may well be subverted by Hurston (she herself would have disowned any such intention or accomplishment). But what has Walker subverted by imitating and so repeating a revisionist moment that she has not originated? No feminist critic will admit the legitimacy of that question, but it abides and will require an answer.

Source: Harold Bloom, ed. *Alice Walker* (New York: Chelsea House, 1989), 1–4.

■ ■ ■ ■ ■ ■ ■ ■ ■ ■ ■ ■ ■ ■ ■ ■ ■

Having Students Take a Critical Stance: Suggested Essay Topics

■ Assign to groups of students essays from *In Search of Our Mothers' Garden: Womanist Prose* to read and discuss. The following essays are a good place to start: "That Is Your Own: The Importance of Models in the Artist's Life," "Looking for Zora," and "The Civil Rights Movement: What Good Was It?" Next, have students individually write a paper exploring their reaction to Walker's essay. Do they agree or disagree with what she has said here? Remind students that they must support their opinions with evidence.

■ Ask students to write an essay that explores Alice Walker's use of figurative language. How has Walker employed metaphor, simile, personification, and other literary devices in her work? Require that students include in their essays the definitions of any literary terminology that they use and that they cite from specific poems. This assignment is excellent for teaching students how to quote poetry within the body of an essay.

■ During the sixties young people voiced loud and sometimes violent protests against the war in Vietnam and racial injustice. Many of these young people are now powerful adults shaping American policy. After researching the student activist movement, have students write about how this movement influences our political thinking today.

■ Have students choose one of Alice Walker's collections of poetry and write a review for the school newspaper of this volume. What poems would they recommend to other students? What is there about Walker's work that would appeal to other teenage writers? Is there anything about Walker's work that might repel some readers?

■ Ask students to choose a poem of Alice Walker's that seems particularly autobiographical. Next, have students write an account of what they think happened in the poet's life to inspire such a poem. Encourage students to speculate but not wildly. They must be able to point to some evidence in the poem to support their speculations.

■ Pair poems from Alice Walker's early and late work; for example, pair "Revolutionary Petunias" (1970) with "A Woman Is Not a Potted Plant" (1991), or "Be Nobody's Darling" (1970) with "The Awakening" (1991). All of these poems and many more that would be interesting to compare can be found in the collection *Her Blue Body Everything We Know*. Have students write a comparison and contrast paper focusing on the ways in which Alice Walker's poetry has evolved over time. What aspects of her style and content have remained constant? Which have changed?

■ Read Zora Neale Hurston's *Their Eyes Were Watching God* and have students compare their response to Janie Crawford's character with Alice Walker's as portrayed in her poem "Janie Crawford" from *Good Night, Willie Lee.*

> **Janie Crawford**
> *Alice Walker*
>
> i love the way Janie Crawford
>
> left her husbands   the one who wanted
> to change her into a mule
> and the other who tried to interest her
> in being a queen
> a woman unless she submits is neither a mule
> nor a queen
> though like a mule she may suffer
> and like a queen pace
> the floor (18)

5 Censorship

■ ■

Along with being one of the most written-about contemporary authors, Alice Walker is also one of the most often censored. According to the Office for Intellectual Freedom, the American Library Association (ALA), and The People for the American Way, *The Color Purple* was recently

- challenged as an appropriate reading for an Oakland, California high school honors class (1984) due to the work's "sexual and social explicitness" and its "troubling ideas about race relations, man's relationship to God, African history and human sexuality." After months of haggling and delays, a divided Oakland Board of Education gave formal approval for the book's use.

- rejected for purchase by the Hayward, California, school trustees (1985) because of "rough language" and "explicit sex scenes."

- removed from the open shelves of the Newport News, Virginia, school library (1986) because of its "profanity and sexual references" and because the school principal felt it "might incite rape." The book was restricted to a special section accessible only to students over the age of eighteen or those who have written permission from a parent.

I believe the following statement on intellectual freedom issued by the National Council of Teachers of English and the International Reading Association should be engraved on every classroom door:

> All students in public school classrooms have the right to materials and educational experiences that promote open inquiry, critical thinking, diversity in thought and expression, and respect for others. Denial or restriction of this right is an infringement of intellectual freedom.

Often when people object to books such as *The Color Purple* they do so on the basis of particular lines or expressions that some find offensive. The more our students understand character motivation, historical context, and diction at the service of tone, the better they will be able to articulate to anyone intent upon protecting them from such books why the author chose to employ this language. I believe that strong, thoughtful students are one of the best defenses against censorship.

Rather than avoiding particular books to stave off the headache and heartache of a challenge, teachers should be proactive in developing clear rationales for the literature they teach. Fortunately, much of the work has been done for us. The National Council of Teachers of English in partnership with the International Reading Association has created a compact disc called *Rationales for Challenged Books*. The CD-ROM was written primarily for middle and high school teachers and includes over two hundred rationales. It also includes references to reviews, plot summaries, redeeming qualities, teaching objectives, and model assignments. The following rationale for teaching *The Color Purple* was prepared by the ALA Intellectual Freedom Committee.

Reading and re-reading *The Color Purple,* one passage seems to illuminate the intent or purpose of Walker's story of two sisters, bound to each other by love and fear, joy and sorrow, and reunited after a separation of thirty years, "He laugh. Who you think you is? He say. You can't curse nobody. Look at you. You black, you pore, you ugly, you a woman. Goddam, he say, you nothing at all." (*The Color Purple,* 176)

That is what people fear and despise in this book. For people who believe, implicitly that to be black/poor/ugly/woman is to be nothing—and to be all of these together is to be less than nothing, the lowest thing in Creation—Walker's book is political, social and sexual heresy.

For Walker is blaspheming against the accepted order of things. She is daring to say that you can be black/poor/ugly/woman and you are nonetheless somebody, a person of intrinsic dignity and worth. There is no such thing as "trash" if you believe, and practice the belief (in Shug's words) that God is not He or She but It, and that it is everywhere and in everything. "I'm pore, I'm black, I may be ugly and can't cook, a voice says to everything listening. But I'm here." (*The Color Purple,* 176)

There is noting new or shocking in the elements of Walker's narrative. We have heard all of these stories before. It is the angle of approach that is so unsettling. We have all heard about oppression from the point of view of the oppressors, about racial relations from the dominant race, about religion from those who preach God the Old Man, about marriage from husbands and sex from men. But in *The Color Purple* we view these familiar conflicts from the other perspective, from the inside out and the bottom up, and what we are forced to see is painful indeed.

Yet out of violence, poverty, oppression and abuse, Celie creates a life for herself and reaches out with love to those around her. Out of all she has experienced she emerges strong and enduring. Quilting is the metaphor for this process of growth in the book: Celie takes the ragged scraps of her life and pieces them together with exquisite stitches into a pattern of beauty. For Walker, Celie's life, like her quilts, is beautiful and precious because of the time and effort, the thought and care, which have gone into its making.

Understanding why someone might object to a piece of literature can help a teacher construct her own personal rationale for choosing to teach a particular novel. Most challenges begin with a phone call from a parent. If the teacher who responds to that call can articulate a thoughtful explanation of why the book is being studied and then offer the child alternate selections, the problem is often diffused. As Louann Reid explains, "Paradoxically, it may take a village to raise a child, but it seems to take only one complaint to raze a curriculum. Reports from organizations such as People for the American Way and the American Library Association demonstrate that challenges to teaching materials and methods are increasing—and are increasingly successful"

Every teacher should expect, at some time in his or her career, to face a textbook challenge. While the circumstances of the challenge and the nature of the objections may be outside a teacher's control, there is much we can do to defend our students' right to read and our own right to teach. My best advice is not to go it alone. Help is always available from the National Council of Teachers of English.

6 More . . .

■■■■■■■■■■■■■■■■■■■■■■■■■■■■■■■■■■

If I could own only one volume of poetry by Alice Walker, it would be her collection *Her Blue Body Everything We Know,* published by Harcourt Brace Jovanovich (1991). Most "selected poems" volumes are published because a poet's early books have gone out of print. This is not the case with Walker, yet I still find it enormously valuable to have selections from four of her books as well as previously uncollected poems all gathered in one place. The collection also offers a clear record of Walker's evolution as a writer.

For my classroom library, I love to use the slim, individual volumes of poetry. My library would be incomplete without the following collections by Alice Walker:

■ *Once: Poems,* paperback.1968. New York: Harcourt Brace Jovanovich.

■ *Revolutionary Petunias,* paperback. 1970. New York: Harcourt Brace Jovanovich.

■ *Good Night, Willie Lee, I'll See You in the Morning,* paperback. 1979. New York: Harcourt Brace Jovanovich.

■ *Horses Make a Landscape More Beautiful,* paperback. 1983. New York: Harcourt Brace Jovanovich.

Other, Highly Recommended Works by Alice Walker

In Search of Our Mothers' Gardens: Womanist Prose. New York: Harcourt
 Brace Jovanovich, 1982.

This early collection of Walker's nonfiction chronicles the turbulent 60s
and 70s as seen through the eyes of a visionary black woman. Throughout this volume, Walker explores the theories and practices of feminists
and feminism.

Living by the Word. New York: Harcourt Brace Jovanovich, 1988.

These essays from 1973–1987 explore feminist, environmental, and political issues, shedding new light on racial debates including the controversy surrounding *The Color Purple.*

The Same River Twice: Honoring the Difficult. New York: Harcourt Brace
 Jovanovich, 1996.

Walker's subtitle for this book is "A Meditation on Life, Spirit, Art, and
the Making of the Film *The Color Purple,* ten years later." It is essential
reading for anyone interested in exploring complex relationships among
artists working together on a project.

Anything We Love Can Be Saved: A Writer's Activism. New York: Harcourt
 Brace Jovanovich, 1997.

In a series of nonfiction articles, Walker writes about her life as an activist. Using her own experiences as examples, she demonstrates how the
world can be saved if only people will act.

Recordings

Two extraordinary audio recordings of interviews with Alice
Walker are available:

■ *Alice Walker, My Life as Myself,* available from Sounds True Audio, 735 Walnut Street, Boulder, Colorado 80302. On this tape

Alice Walker takes you into her private world and talks about fighting oppression with creativity.

■ *Alice Walker, The World Is Made of Stories,* available from New Dimensions Foundation, P.O. Box 410510, San Francisco, California 94141. In two interviews with Justine and Michael Toms, Walker speaks of the need to free ourselves from oppression as well as the need to celebrate the fullness of life.

Videotape
The Lannan Foundation has created a powerful sixty-minute video that combines Alice Walker's Lannan Literary Award with an interview at her home in northern California by the journalist Evelyn White. The tape is available from the Lannan Foundation, 5401 McConnell Avenue, Los Angeles, California 90066.

After watching this video, my student Betty Rosas wrote, "Alice Walker is a very invigorating woman, full of ideas that make me proud to be a woman. Hearing her read her poems and watching her expressions as she read and seeing what a beautiful person she is just made me want to read more."

Chronology of Alice Walker's Life

■■■■■■■■■■■■■■■■■■■■■■■■■■■■■■■■

1944   Born on February 9, in Eatonton, Georgia, to Willie
        Lee and Minnie Tallulah Walker. She is the eighth and
        last child born in this sharecropping family.

1952   Alice Walker is injured in an accident with a BB gun
        and as a result loses sight in one eye. Scar tissue grows
        over the eye causing the young girl to become extremely
        self-conscious and withdrawn, unable to look people
        in the eye.

1958   Through surgery, the scar tissue on Walker's eye is re-
        moved.

1961–65 Walker enrolls at Spelman College, an elite college for
        black women. Two years later she transferred to Sarah
        Lawrence. Traveling to Africa for a summer, Walker
        begins to write poetry. Muriel Rukeyser was an early
        mentor.

1967   Walker marries Melvyn Roseman Levanthal, a civil
        rights lawyer. They move to Mississippi to work.

1968   *Once*, Walker's first book of poetry is published.

1969   Daughter, Rebecca, is born.

1970   Walker's first novel, *The Third Life of Grange Copeland*, is published.

1973   Walker is awarded the National Book Award for the collection *Revolutionary Petunias*.

1974   Walker receives the Rosenthal Foundation Award from the American Academy of Arts and Letters for *In Love and Trouble: Stories of Black Women*.

1975   Walker becomes a contributing editor to *Ms. Magazine*.

1976   *Meridian,* Walker's second novel, is published. She and Levanthal divorce.

1979   Walker publishes the collection *Good Night, Willie Lee, I'll See You in the Morning* and moves to California to begin to write *The Color Purple*.

1981   A second collection of stories, *You Can't Keep a Good Woman Down,* is published.

1981   *The Color Purple* is published, garnering a nomination for a National Book Critics Circle Award. Walker is named a distinguished writer in Afro-American Studies at Berkeley.

1982   *The Color Purple* receives the Pulitzer Prize. Walker publishes *In Search of Our Mothers' Gardens*, a book of "womanist" prose.

1983   *Horses Make a Landscape More Beautiful,* a poetry collection, is published.

1984   Premier of the movie *The Color Purple* in Eatonton, Georgia, on January 18.

1988   *Living by the Word,* a volume of essays, appears.

1989   Walker publishes *The Temple of My Familiar.*

1990   *Finding the Green Stone* and *Her Blue Body Everything We Know: Earthling Poems 1965–1990* are published.

1991   *Possessing the Secret of Joy* is published.

1992   Walker publishes *Warrior Marks: Female Genital Mutilation and the Sexual Blinding of Women.* The film *Warrior Marks* debuts.

1996   *The Same River Twice: Honoring the Difficult* is published, recounting the story of the making of the film *The Color Purple.*

1997   A collection of essays recounting Walker's activism, *Anything We Love Can Be Saved,* is published.

1998   *By the Light of My Father's Smile,* a novel, is published.

Works Cited

■ ■

BIRKERTS, SVEN. *The Gutenberg Elegies: The Fate of Reading in an Electronic Age.* New York: Fawcett Columbine, 1994.

BLOOM, HAROLD, ed. *Alice Walker.* New York: Chelsea House Publishers, 1989.

BRODSKY, JOSEPH. "Nobel Lecture." *Nobel e-Museum.* Last modified on June 1, 2000. http://www.nobel.se/literature/laureates/1987/brodsky-lecture.html (May 1999).

The Color Purple. Dir. Steven Spielberg. Perf. Danny Glover, Whoopi Goldberg, Margaret Avery, Oprah Winfrey, Adolph Caesar. Warner Bros., 1985.

EPSTEIN, JOSEPH, ed. *The Norton Book of Personal Essays.* New York: W.W. Norton, 1997.

JOHNSON, MARIA V. "'You Just Can't Keep a Good Woman Down': Alice Walker Sings the Blues." *sistahspace.* 1996. http://www.sistahspace.com/sistory/writers/walker/youjust.html (May 1999).

MACKEY, MARGARET. "Good Enough Reading: Momentum and Accuracy in the Reading of Complex Fiction." *Research in the Teaching of English* 31, 4 (December 1997): 428–58.

PRICE, DEB. "Alice through the Looking Glass." *Detroit News* 1 March 1996.

Rationales for Challenged Books. National Council of Teachers of English in partnership with the International Reading Association. Urbana: National Council of Teachers of English, 1998.

ROSENBLATT, LOUISE. *Literature as Exploration.* New York: The Modern Language Association, 1983.

WALKER, ALICE. "Beauty: When the Other Dancer Is the Self," *In Search of Our Mother's Gardens: Womanist Prose*. New York: Harcourt Brace Jovanovich, 1983.

———. *The Color Purple*. New York: Washington Square Press, 1982.

———. *Good Night, Willie Lee, I'll See You in the Morning*. New York: Harcourt Brace Jovanovich, 1979.

———. *Her Blue Body Everything We Know: Earthling Poems, 1965–1990*. San Diego: Harcourt Brace Jovanovich, 1991.

———. *Living by the Word*. New York: Harcourt Brace Jovanovich, 1988.

———. *In Love and Trouble: Stories of Black Women*. New York: Harcourt Brace Jovanovich, 1974.

———. *The Same River Twice: Honoring the Difficult*. New York: Scribner, 1996.

———. *In Search of Our Mother's Gardens: Womanist Prose*. New York: Harcourt Brace Jovanovich, 1982.

WHITAKER, CHARLES. "Alice Walker: *Color Purple* Author Confronts Her Critics and Talks about Her Provocative New Book." *Ebony Magazine* 47, no. 7 (May 1992): 86–90.

Author

Carol Jago teaches English at Santa Monica High School in Santa Monica, California, and directs the California Reading and Literature Project at UCLA. She is editor of *California English,* the quarterly journal of the California Association of Teachers of English (CATE). Jago also writes a weekly education column for the *Los Angeles Times.* Her essays have appeared in *English Journal, Language Arts, NEA Today, The Christian Science Monitor,* and other newspapers across the nation. She has been director of the NCTE Commission on Literature and currently serves on the Secondary Section of the Executive Committee of the National Council of Teachers of English. She is the author of *Nikki Giovanni in the Classroom: "The same ol' danger but a brand new pleasure"* and *With Rigor for All: Teaching the Classics to Contemporary Students.*

This book was typeset in Berkeley and Interstate
by Electronic Imaging.

The typefaces used on the cover were Helvetica, Zurich Ex Bt,
and Albertus Medium.

The book was printed on 50-lb. Husky Offset by
IPC Communication Services.